Brands We Know

Netflix

By Sara Green

Bellwether Media • Minneapolis, MN

Jump into the cockpit and take flight with Pilot books. Your journey will take you on high-energy adventures as you learn about all that is wild, weird, fascinating, and fun!

This edition first published in 2018 by Bellwether Media, Inc.

Library of Congress Cataloging-in-Publication Data

Names: Green, Sara, 1964- author.
Title: Netflix / by Sara Green.
Description: Minneapolis, MN : Bellwether Media, Inc., [2018] | Series:
  Pilot: Brands We Know | Includes bibliographical references and
  index. | Audience: Grades 3-8
Identifiers: LCCN 2017012074 (print) | LCCN 2016052745 (ebook) |
  ISBN 9781626176539 (hardcover : alk. paper) | ISBN 9781681033839
  (ebook)
Subjects: LCSH: Netflix (Firm)--Juvenile literature. | Video rental
  services--United States--Juvenile literature. | Internet videos--United
  States--Juvenile literature. | Streaming technology
  (Telecommunications)--Juvenile literature.
Classification: LCC HD9697.V544 N48275 2018 (ebook) | LCC HD9697.
  V544 (print) | DDC 384.55/506573--dc23
LC record available at https://lccn.loc.gov/2017012074

Editor: Betsy Rathburn   Designer: Josh Brink

Printed in the United States of America, North Mankato, MN.

NETFLIX

Table of Contents

What Is Netflix?

The Saturday night sleepover has begun! A group of friends eats pizza and plays games. Later, they will watch a movie on Netflix. Some kids want to watch *Minions*. Others prefer *Zootopia* or *The Jungle Book*. With so many movies to choose from, picking one is difficult. Can the friends stay awake long enough to watch all three?

Netflix, Inc. is an American entertainment company. Its **headquarters** is in Los Gatos, California. Netflix offers a popular **subscription** video service. It **streams** movies and television shows online. It also mails DVDs and Blu-ray discs to members. People use Netflix **apps** to watch movies and TV episodes on their mobile devices. Today, more than 100 million people around the world subscribe to Netflix. It is one of the most popular media **brands** on Earth!

Minions

By the Numbers

more than
100 million
Netflix members

42.5 billion
hours spent
streaming Netflix
in 2015

more than
300
original programs
by 2017

members
located in
190
countries

3,700
Netflix employees

available in
22
languages

Netflix headquarters, Los Gatos, California

A Business Brainstorm

Netflix began in 1997. Two men, Reed Hastings and Marc Randolph, **founded** the company in Scotts Valley, California. Both men had already achieved success before starting Netflix. Reed was a computer scientist. He started a business called Pure **Software** in 1991. In time, Reed's company combined with another to create a large company called Pure Atria.

Marc had also started other businesses before Netflix. He met Reed when Pure Atria bought one of Marc's businesses. The two men soon became friends. They enjoyed discussing ideas for new businesses.

Marc Randolph

Reed Hastings

In the mid-1990s, DVDs were invented. They were smaller and more lightweight than earlier home video options. This made them easy to ship to people's houses. At the same time, use of the Internet was growing. Ordering items online was becoming common. This gave Reed and Marc an idea. They could start an online DVD rental business!

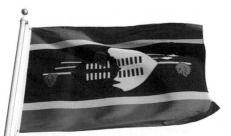

Peace Corps Volunteer

After graduating from college, Reed Hastings joined the Peace Corps. He taught math in a small African country called Swaziland for more than two years.

Reed sold Pure Atria for $750 million in 1997. He was now ready to start a new business. He and Marc decided to create the DVD rental service they had discussed. Reed invested about $2 million to get Netflix started. The company started with 30 employees. There were 925 movie titles to choose from.

In the beginning, Netflix tried different payment systems. It soon settled on a subscription service. Members created lists of movies they wanted to watch. Netflix mailed the DVDs to their homes. Afterwards, members mailed the DVDs back in a Netflix envelope. Netflix even paid

for postage. People no longer had to rent movies at video stores. There were also no late fees! Soon, Netflix added another service. It began suggesting movies members might like based on their tastes. People could now discover movies they might have missed otherwise!

Name Game

The word Netflix is a combination of two words. "Net" comes from "Internet," and "flix" comes from "flicks," a term for movies.

Netflix Grows

Netflix gained members quickly. It had one million members by early 2003. Business deals with movie studios helped Netflix increase its DVD library. Many of these DVDs were not available in video stores. This helped Netflix boost its membership numbers. By 2005, the company had 35,000 film titles available. It was shipping around one million DVDs every day! Around this time, Netflix lost an important member. Marc left in 2004 to start another company.

Big Dream
DreamWorks was one of the first movie studios to make a deal with Netflix.

Netflix took a major step in 2007. It added the online video streaming option. Netflix members could still receive DVDs. But they could also stream movies and television shows from the Internet. They watched the programs on their computers and televisions. The next year, members could also stream onto their mobile devices. Streaming allowed people to easily watch many episodes in a row. Best of all, there were no commercials! Soon, people in other countries could also enjoy Netflix. The company expanded to Latin America and the Caribbean in 2011. Over the next three years, Netflix also became available in many countries in Europe.

By 2011, business was booming for Netflix. It had beaten all of its competition. It was the top DVD-by-mail Internet business in the world. Its streaming service was also becoming more popular. More than 20 million people were Netflix members at this time.

Snail Mail

Netflix is one of the largest users of the U.S. Postal Service. More than 4 million people receive Netflix DVDs through the mail.

But even the most successful companies can make mistakes. In the summer of 2011, Reed announced plans to divide the company. One part would focus on streaming. The other would be dedicated to mailing DVDs. The company would also raise its prices. Many members were upset by the news. Within months, Netflix lost 800,000 customers. Some people worried that Netflix would end forever. Reed realized he had made a mistake. He decided not to make the changes. Slowly, customers returned to Netflix. But could Netflix bounce back?

Original Hits

Netflix took another big step in 2013. The company began to offer original content for its members. The first series was a **drama** for adults called *House of Cards*. The show was a huge hit. Over time, Netflix continued to release more original programs. *All Hail King Julien* and *Turbo FAST* drew in younger viewers. Netflix also brought Marvel superheroes to life. These included Jessica Jones, Luke Cage, and Daredevil. People loved these shows. Netflix was on top once again!

Netflix has found great success with its original programs. By 2017, there were more than 300 original programs on Netflix. Over time, many of these programs have won awards. *House of Cards* and *Jessica Jones* are two popular trophy winners. In 2017, *The White Helmets* won Netflix its first **Academy Award**!

Count Olaf

Secrets Will Be Revealed

Netflix debuted *A Series of Unfortunate Events* in 2017. The series follows three orphans as they try to escape the evil Count Olaf.

Netflix Originals for Kids

Justin

Grug Crood

Name of Program	Debut Year
Justin Time GO!	2011
Dragons: Race to the Edge	2012
Turbo FAST	2013
All Hail King Julien	2014
VeggieTales in the House	2014
Dawn of the Croods	2015
Dinotrux	2015
H2O: Mermaid Adventures	2015
Richie Rich	2015
Degrassi: Next Class	2016
Kong: King of the Apes	2016
Kulipari: An Army of Frogs	2016
Voltron: Legendary Defender	2016
A Series of Unfortunate Events	2017

Kong

Turbo

Ty T-Trux

What's On Today?

Today, Netflix is more popular than ever. It has more than 100 million members in 190 countries around the world. Netflix's DVD rental **division** is now called DVD.com. Members can rent movies through the web site to watch at home. *Trolls* and *Brave* are popular rental choices.

Netflix's streaming library includes other great choices for kids. Star Wars fans follow favorite characters by streaming *Star Wars: The Clone Wars*. **Documentaries** take members on journeys across the globe. *Planet Earth* and *Life* are popular options. Netflix also offers another bonus to streamers. It is the only service in the United States with the **rights** to stream all new Disney movies!

Star Wars: The Clone Wars

Discover new stories.
current tagline

The Defenders

Netflix continues to launch new original programs. In 2017, *The Defenders* brought Marvel superheroes together to battle enemies. *Spy Kids: Mission Critical* and *Hilda* **debuted** in 2018. These series follow kids on their exciting adventures. Even more programs are in the works. In the future, half of Netflix's total content will likely be original!

17

Netflix Extras

Netflix leaders believe in helping others. In 2016, Reed Hastings used $100 million of his own money to start a **foundation** called the Hastings Fund. This organization is committed to improving education. In its first year, the fund gave more than $1 million to help people attend college. The foundation also supports other causes. It donated $50,000 to the **ACLU** in 2017. This organization defends the rights of all Americans.

Netflix gives back in other ways, too. The company matches its employees' donations to many **charities** up to $10,000 per year! The company also offers a service called **audio** description. It allows people with poor eyesight to enjoy Netflix programs. A **narrator** explains what is happening on screen. This technology is also available on Netflix's web sites and apps. Netflix wants to make education and entertainment accessible to everyone!

Netflix Narrator

Netflix has more than 300 programs with audio description available!

Because great things start with Netflix.

2010s tagline

Netflix Holiday Gift Program to raise money for Feeding America

19

Netflix Timeline

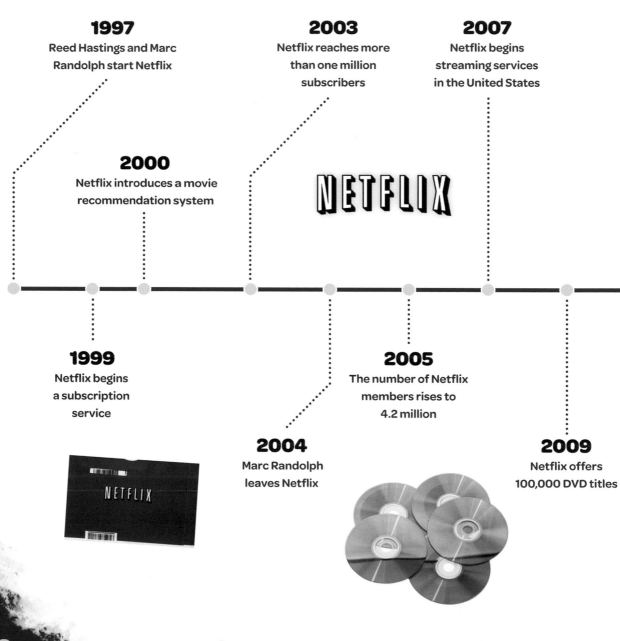

1997
Reed Hastings and Marc Randolph start Netflix

2000
Netflix introduces a movie recommendation system

2003
Netflix reaches more than one million subscribers

2007
Netflix begins streaming services in the United States

1999
Netflix begins a subscription service

2005
The number of Netflix members rises to 4.2 million

2004
Marc Randolph leaves Netflix

2009
Netflix offers 100,000 DVD titles

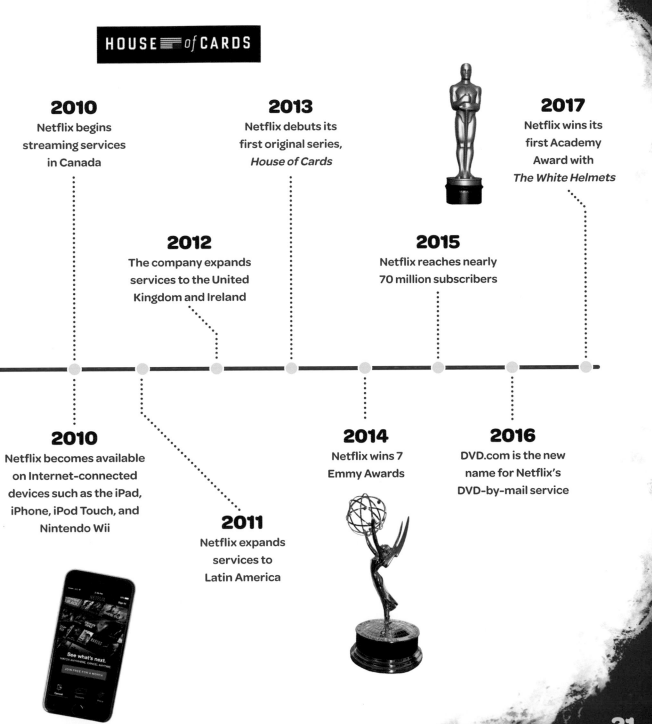

HOUSE *of* **CARDS**

2010
Netflix begins
streaming services
in Canada

2013
Netflix debuts its
first original series,
House of Cards

2017
Netflix wins its
first Academy
Award with
The White Helmets

2012
The company expands
services to the United
Kingdom and Ireland

2015
Netflix reaches nearly
70 million subscribers

2010
Netflix becomes available
on Internet-connected
devices such as the iPad,
iPhone, iPod Touch, and
Nintendo Wii

2014
Netflix wins 7
Emmy Awards

2016
DVD.com is the new
name for Netflix's
DVD-by-mail service

2011
Netflix expands
services to
Latin America

Glossary

Academy Award—a yearly award presented for achievement in film; an Academy Award is also called an Oscar.

ACLU—American Civil Liberties Union

apps—small, specialized programs downloaded onto smartphones and other mobile devices

audio—sound

brands—categories of products all made by the same company

charities—organizations that help others in need

debuted—was introduced for the first time

division—a separate part of a business

documentaries—movies or television shows that show real-life events

drama—a performance for entertainment that is serious and does not make an audience laugh

foundation—an institution that provides funds to charitable organizations

founded—created a company

headquarters—a company's main office

narrator—the person who tells a story

rights—the legal ability to use a certain name or product

software—a program that tells a computer what to do

streams—sends or receives video and audio material over the Internet

subscription—an arrangement for regularly providing a service in exchange for money

To Learn More

AT THE LIBRARY

Garza, Sarah. *Action! Making Movies*. Huntington Beach, Calif.: Teacher Created Materials, 2013.

Green, Sara. *Disney*. Minneapolis, Minn.: Bellwether Media, 2014.

Hunter, Nick. *Showtime!: The Entertainment Industry*. New York, N.Y.: Gareth Stevens Publishing, 2013.

ON THE WEB

Learning more about Netflix is as easy as 1, 2, 3.

1. Go to www.factsurfer.com.

2. Enter "Netflix" into the search box.

3. Click the "Surf" button and you will see a list of related web sites.

With factsurfer.com, finding more information is just a click away.

Index

The images in this book are reproduced through the courtesy of: Christopher Hall, front cover (popcorn bucket left); Josh Brink, front cover (King Julien logo, Ever After High logos, Turbo FAST logo, Voltron logo, Dragon Race logo), p. 15 (all); stevepb, front cover (popcorn bits); Paul Stringer, front cover (tablet, phone); Aptyp_koK, front cover (DVD case); Dynamicfoto, front cover (remote control); Stiftelsen Elektronikkbransjen/ Flickr, front cover (television); Marit & Toomas Hinnosaar/ Flickr, front cover (Netflix envelope); sharpshutter, front cover (popcorn bucket right); Ttatty, front cover (laptop); ibreakstock, p. 4 (bottom left); AF archive/ Alamy, p. 4 (bottom left); Jason Doiy, p. 5 (building); lolya1988, p. 5 (sky); ENRIQUE GARCÍA MEDINA/ Newscom, p. 6; FERNANDO MASSOBRIO/ Newscom, p. 7 (top); railway fx, p. 7 (bottom); Marianna Day Massey/ ZUMA Press, p. 8; Justin Sullivan/ Getty Images, p. 9; Kristoffer Tripplaar/ Alamy, p. 10; sitthiphong, p. 11; Ricardo Ramirez Buxeda/ Newscom, p. 12; STEVE MARCUS/ Newscom, p. 13; Kred, PacificCoastNews/ Newscom, p. 14; Singapore/ LucasFilm/ Newscom, p. 16; Steve Sands/ Getty Images, p. 17; Nata-Lia, p. 18; Antonio de Moraes Barros Filho WireImage/ Getty Images, p. 19; emptyclouds, p. 20 (bottom left); yurchello108, p. 20 (bottom right); Netflix Media Center/ Wikipedia, p. 20 (top); Wikipedia, p. 21 (top left); Joe Seer, p. 21 (bottom right); ArthurStock, p. 21 (bottom left); s_bukley, p. 21 (top right).